How To Find All Missing Persons / Unsolved Cases. And Collect All Reward Offers. Volume XV. THE CASE OF GWENNETH GRAHAM

DAVID GOMADZA

www.twofuture.world

Copyright © 2024 David Gomadza

All rights reserved.

Paperback ISBN: 9798326749048

DEDICATION

To a better futures

CONTENTS

How To Find All Missing Persons /
Unsolved Cases.
And Collect All Reward Offers. Volume XV
THE CASE OF GWENNETH GRAHAM   1

The Afterlife Conversation

and The Council Of Creation.   6

The Killers.   16

ACKNOWLEDGMENTS

Tomorrow's World Order

How To Find All Missing Persons / Unsolved Cases. And Collect All Reward Offers. Volume XV. THE CASE OF GWENNETH GRAHAM

BACKGROUND INFORMATION

CASE

CATEGORY

$1m Reward, Cold Cases

DATE

27 Sep 1974

DESCRIPTION:

46 years of age.

5 feet 2 inches (157 cm) tall.

Medium build.

How To Find All Missing Persons / Unsolved Cases. And Collect All Reward Offers.
Volume XV. THE CASE OF GWENNETH GRAHAM

Wavy brown hair.

QUICK CASE FACTS:

Gwenneth Graham lived with her husband in Balga.

Last seen leaving the Malthouse Tavern around 11:15pm on Friday 27 September 1974.

Reported missing on 1 October 1974.

Body located by two young boys in bushland off Balga Avenue, Balga on Sunday 6 October 1974.

BACKGROUND:

Gwenneth Graham was born Gwenneth Murray in May 1928. She lived in Balga with her husband.

Balga is a suburb of Perth, Western Australia and is located approximately 13km north of the Perth Central Business District.

CASE DETAILS:

Mrs Graham was seen around 11:15pm leaving the Malthouse Tavern, Balga on Friday 27 September 1974. Both the WAFL and VFL football grand finals were played the following day.

Mrs Graham was reported missing, by her husband, on Tuesday 1 October 1974.

LOCATED:

Around 10.30am on Sunday October 6, 1974 the body of Mrs Graham was located by two young boys in a bush area surrounded by Balga Avenue, Heyshot Road, Climping Street and Walderton Avenue, Balga.

A number of items were located near the body including some money and a packet of cigarettes.

The person or persons responsible for Mrs Graham's murder have not yet been identified.

TOMORROW'S WORLD ORDER'S PERSPECTIVES

USE OF PREDEFINED AFTERLIFE PARAMETERS

These guide souls the moment it exist the human body on its journey to Yahweh the creator these define what to do and what to expect as you go to hell or heaven if a souk leaves earth it enters ozone orbit and instantly everything reboots for it to start a new phase of life after living the earth's body now what happens is that it enters the ozone orbit and a simply click caused by the sudden drop of pressure from -1186 to – 20 means the bottom shaft of the soul will lift rapidly and this pushes its back into the air higher than its head best example is a penguin but with real human legs and head just the shape now God created a life predefined program for them instead of asking what should I do and where should I go they instantly know from predefined stencils if you did well and talked most about God then heaven is for you if you did evil and talked more about the devil then the devil is yours now if we Ask what can be of humans without souks this is the answer dead forever your soul is you a new transformation to the electromagnetic waves life where you see Yahweh for the first time and praise him and wish you had seen him a long time ago because of his Majesty and will always be there forever now what are all these you may ask these are rules to be guided by in the creation court in short it has everything humans know about the judges and the presiding judge who will always be Yahweh and 84 angels surrounding the altar 28 high priests who always say Yahweh have mercy on humans and 74 smaller courts priests who always say Yahweh has mercy on humans and 96 princesses who say glory to Yahweh forever and ever amen we have 96 elders who always say if I can why he can't meaning if the devil can drink blood why can't Yahweh who created the devil and blood do the same now this is not the same as saying if the devil can kill why can Yahweh its more on professional grounds rather than challenging now if we look at the inside of the court we have 81 priests surrounding the altar who say Yahweh be merciful to humans but if they disobey you we put hem on trial for you and kill them for you almighty Yahweh inside this is a round circle where Yahweh sits and asks questions now if we look deep inside the court you will see that there are other things that resemble earth high courts like benches and chairs 10 times human sizes for the gods who are so enormous 2 are equal to 84 billion humans in size predefined parameters for humans after death as in know what is inside is a large size of books the book of creation is among them with 10897867892836789012348678901245861789011 pages and is divided into humans first then chapter for animals then a chapter for angles then a chapter for gods and a chapter for Joseph Yahweh's best friend and a chapter for Yahweh's best friend's wife Anna and a chapter for Yahweh's wife Catitighit and lastly a chapter for Yahweh and recently a chapter for davidgomadza as Yahweh's representative on earth marking the new beginnings starting in 2025

1. tell us who killed you
2. tell us what killed you
3. tell us why and who killed you
4. tell us why you died
5. tell us what could have been done and is not done
6. tell us what could be and why
7. tell is when this happened
8. tell us why this is so
9. tell us why this is so
10. what can be done to improve this

What does the book of creation say about davidgomadza David Gomadza is the first and last ruler to be appointed by Yahweh fir the next 25 billion years and will act as his representative on earth deciding cases and upholding his principles on earth and as such has been entitled to 489 trillion dollars in assets this number signifies eternity among humans and the beginning of a new Era chapter 78678928028938628418902876890183208678901234867890182364872891286
10 Creation manual the new Era of new electromagnetic wave conduit signed and dated by Yahweh himself

on 27may2024 at 237800 Yatime
creation.universe.ya.start.end.find.davidgomadza.ya.askya.ya

Ask.read.creation.manucreation.universe.ya.start.end.find.davidgomaaskya.ya

Ask.rulesofthecourt.start.now.start
David Gomadza welcome the rules of court are guiding principles that tell you what to do and how to do it first you must always say I believe in the court of creation and I shall abide by he rules of this court and shall always do things according to the rules of this court in deciding the cases I am assigned to you must ask what can be done so that you know all your options before making choices the court system will make it easy to check files and ask the outcomes of the decision ask the court the final decision in the case of gwenneth graham she was killed by his real name is matis mutervnop who was 19 extracts from his brain record were used in this court to decide the facts because he had played God and is being punished by Yahweh staying alone for 1800 days for impersonating Yahweh after which he must be sent to prison for killing gwenneth graham.

THE AFTERLIFE CONVERSATION AND THE COUNCIL OF CREATION'S ANAYLSIS.

GWENNETH GRAHAM

i got attacked by two young boys who i knew and lived locally not for sex but for being grumpy old lady i was 46 at the time and i ignored them for a long time they followed me to where i was and said miss why you so grumpy i did not say anything i moved on until i reached a place that said welcome to atrest and i sat down and one said can you ask me anything and i will tell you and i said okay what is 10 minus 2 and he said in your face old grumpy mrs and i

How To Find All Missing Persons / Unsolved Cases. And Collect All Reward Offers. Volume XV. THE CASE OF GWENNETH GRAHAM

said it's growing up when your balls starts to grow then you will understand and he said i understand but sometimes you need to tell me exactly what i want to hear and i said okay then the other one i assumed was the quiet one said if they can they i can but me for free they steal property killing all orphans and we are all orphans and have property what are chances that we end up dead and i said if you act like you are doing ofcourse you end up dead so i said why not come to my house we talk over a cup of tea and get to know you too and one said okay and the other said what about if i refuse and say maybe you come to my place for sex and i laughed and said this is not how to get women ask nicely then i can give you just once here as long as you are above 16 years and they started crying saying okay that's all we want we mean no trouble what else can you offer us if we don't pay next month they said they will retake the properties so help us with some money where can i get that kind of money i am only 18 and the other said 19 and i said if you had told me a long time ago then i could have helped you now if we come now will you at least give us some we sell one house and payoff the cheapest i agreed now the 19 year old said i can fuck you if you like until we sell the house i said i have a son your size he is coming now i said and they all looked and a big boy started coming towards me and i said wait there there are muggers out here he said these little boys causing problems everywhere and one said if we don't pay they will have to kill us and i said go to the police and he said that's what i meant it's them killing women now my heart tore with fear and i said what can be of these boys and he said killers until the find money they need last week they stabbed a man to death and this week if you don't give them then you will die this week and i refused i said no you know what i don't give in to blackmail and he said then i might start killing you myself i lost my parents to them threatens you must die as well so listen up your money or your life there is no going back on the this one and he stood up and said i can if they can steal and get away why can't i and he raised his hand and sliced me hard that i screamed very hard and one of them kicked me in the head and said you pay or they pay us better if you pay then you have to keep your life but if they pay

How To Find All Missing Persons / Unsolved Cases. And Collect All Reward Offers. Volume XV. THE CASE OF GWENNETH GRAHAM

that means you will be dead i don't want you to die because i want sex with you so today say i can't but then we collect next week i touched chest and i was bleeding heavily and i said take me to the hospital and he said you can't go to the hospital because the doctors will know that we did it which is not good for us so i said you must at least cover the chest with something because if you don't stop the bleeding then i will die fast i was soaked and i realised u was going to die so i took off my blouse and covered my wounds and he said can we now when i was bleeding badly i said no doctor first and he said okay but if i tell you want is to happen you must obey okay and i said yes then he can if i can then he said if you let me know exactly what i can do then let me know because i want you to die in our hands today so that they give us more money if they don't then we are going to keep killing until we finish the neighborhood and get all the houses so the other boy said see your own son stabs you to death this is how bad this has become so i ask last time how much you can spare us then we can talk and have sex and now i was grasping for breath and he said do you know that we can start a war in the city and start killing everyone we are tired of all this and if you don't pay that's it go to heaven where everything is free so i said okay i pay you 400 dollars only then see next month they smiled and said see people understand only violence and i cried and prayed and started hearing praying to Yahweh that went on for sometime then i saw a woman dressed in white and said come this way and i went there and i woke up in heaven now let's analyze the facts of this case this is one of endurance and courage in face of death threats but resulting in death because there has not been been an agreement of what to do now if i ask the highest judge Yahweh what he thinks of this case this is his reply this case is of high importance as it highlight what happens when youth are deprived of opportunities they end up resorting to violence now who killed her is the first question she said my son but it's not her son it's someone who acts as the leader of the group he acts fast and asks critical questions about everything his honesty is unequaled anywhere he is the ultimate cool ruler aiming to take his price with minimum effort now if she wants she can keep the

How To Find All Missing Persons / Unsolved Cases. And Collect All Reward Offers.
Volume XV. THE CASE OF GWENNETH GRAHAM

money but death is imminent she is faced with the choice pay or die now she has no option it's only death as she started hearing singing of people meaning death now how did she die was it that just one slash across the chest if yes then the big boy did it if not then others might have joined in as well now let's look at what happened according to brain scans she died of hearagearomgern meaning loss of blood from the chest area now if we check the long ago start it started at 22.08 local time when it started it started compiling a lot of things namely
   1 time of the incident
   2 the amount of blood lost
   3 the amount of sugar left because sugar is needed for brain functions
4 the amount of oxygen left after the bleeding
5 the amount of sugar per cubic litter of blood
6 the blood levels left
7 the white blood cells
8 the pouride power as a unit
9 the peride power of pore
10 the amount of tar left in the co20z blood oxyh
[ ] now if we ask all these what do they measure this is the answer they measure death by cobs and tells the brain that the cobs of the brain is damaged and must be replaced and fast now what the brain is trying to do is to predict what happens to k where k is the calcium needed to fight off infections by eliminating inaccuracies meaning knowing everything to do with k which means potassium magnet which is needed in case of blood loss which is the luckily cause of death because lack of this means no oxygen being sent to the brain and meant if we remove this k then it's imminent death now if this is added in large quanties doe this mean no death to some extent yes because more of these means more of blood with oxygen going to the brain now if we look at what happened to her then we can see that the man deliberately killed her by a single slash to the chest but that is of not to say that this is the only cause of death there could be other reasons still not known to us so we ask is this what only happened was there other events that led to

How To Find All Missing Persons / Unsolved Cases. And Collect All Reward Offers. Volume XV. THE CASE OF GWENNETH GRAHAM

her death we know for sure that there were others especially those who wanted sex did they not pursue and if they did then at what time now the court of creation must determine at what precise time did the others join if they did if not then she would have had died it take a normal human being about 8 minutes to die from loss of blood and she was slashed at exactly 22.07 pm going home from work now her time of death according to brain scan is 22.23 meaning an extra an extra 7 minus from what we would have expected now let's look at what can be done at this moment in town she could be dying and them pressing for money and sex as things were she was destined to die slashing someone like that and ignore her was meant to kill only but the question that comes to mind is that where we're the police in all this and now we look at how they had deliberately targeted orphans who had houses deposed them and got them killed easily now if we look what could have been then this is the answer the police have meant unlawful acts because if they can kill and get away with it why can anyone as a challenge now everyone started asking if they can then what can stop them from doing the same there is no justification for doing that they were abusing their position to gain unfavorably now what can be said about this case she was targeted by muggers for monthly withdraws of which she agreed to a one of 400 but only after being slashed that in itself is not an act to save oneself because it only came after a dreadful incident but this is not the problem of this case did she send and calls of help to the creator we ask Yahweh she did not the geographical positioning system did not work for her and we ask what happened surely in this case you would expect a message from her inside the first time she screamed [i am your soul i am stuck inside they have used emrt to block the way how can i go out or cry for help how can i go out like this i have emrt all over me if you can tell me them how can i scream this emrt remove all electromagnetic waves now what are these emrt her soul is talking about these are emergency right to tink they are used when there is not enough electromagnetic waves to propel the flight out of soul chamber now why the need for these emrt it's because the slashing has reduced circulation of blood as now most

How To Find All Missing Persons / Unsolved Cases. And Collect All Reward Offers.
Volume XV. THE CASE OF GWENNETH GRAHAM

is being lost to the world and with it goes all electromagnetic waves brought by blood now her body has deployed the emergency exit assist kit emrt that also has not worked because even this require electromagnetic waves but to a lesser extent now if we look closer at this case then we can tell that the emrt had also malfunctioned the electromagnetic level needed for the emrt is so little that they could have worked but even these it's not enough to propel the soul out of the body so it's stuck and say i tried everything gwenneth [gavvino] graham age at death was 46 years slashed on the chest died of anoerestuxis of the body as oxygen lessens as blood loss increased now if we ask her soul it says the body run out of steam there are no electromagnetic waves to deal with instead i keep hearing her say Yahweh come to the rescue where are you why parachute did not open is this supposed to happen did they close it deliberately what we do in situations like this can we escape earth if these crooks have become this clever to start things that jam all your clever plans are they asking who is the real god i want to know and it said i tried so hard to run but as electromagnetic waves how can i when there is not the slightest electromagnetic waves around now what can we learn about this she tried hard to ask for help and even get out but failed if we ask what can be of her then death is the only solution no electromagnetic waves means death for electromagnetic waves driven entity now what other options she had to scream to wake the other creatures that send help calls to Yahweh like the creature on the shoulder or the creature in the stomach that says where is god when awake sending a god.whereareyou.help.now.start now let's look at why this is happening all calls of help have been tampered with now let's ask why is this so had someone tampered with the system if we check we can see that all depends on sufficient electromagnetic waves now why cutting the chest removes all electromagnetic waves did this person know that this is what this does now let's look at what can be there can be another system that don't rely on electromagnetic waves this system can complement this one but what kind could it be and how could that work if we are to put one driven by aerosifine then that will be great because aerosifine is not human but abundant in heaven formula is x=y but y=x then if x is y what is x where x is a consonant but can be changed its chemical formula is x is oxygen plus nitrate plus oxide plus atmospheric pressure at -780 degrees in a pressurized container now if we ask what can this do then we can use it as a propellant to drive everything out fast and secure now if we ask what is to be then this is what can be said of this now let's look at other ways we can do this we can always ask a question what can be done to all this this means we must be in a position to find new ways of calling for help humans now make a call just touch naval and the message is sent now if we ask the court of creation what suggestions they can give us this is their answer they can easily replace all systems with a direct call function that uses electromagnetic waves in a container because in the open it will never work now if we write the code this is what the code will look like x=y

y=x now if x is y then what is y where y is x plus a change that can be a consonant now if x is y then what is y if y is x then what is x as we do this it will come clearer that when x is y then there is a line now if we say x is y then y is x then what is x if x is y then what is x if y is x then what is x now if we substitute x for y then this equation becomes x is x plus x to power 2 plus x to power 3 plus x to power 4 and so on that means if x is y then y is x to the power 2 inverse number is 0.087683210 now if we can construct the system it will say if x is y then y is 0.087683210 now ask what can be done with this equation then this is the answer we can easily ask people what could be done this is the answer we can call Yahweh directly just touch your naval and say i give to Yahweh then the message will be sent to Yahweh now what is to be of human humans will be humans and will always need Yahweh forever now what is to be is to be Yahweh can and will always be there for humans humans can thank Yahweh now let's ask why the system did not deploy itself to the creator himself humans are learning ways to defeat their creator that means doing everything right for the wrong reasons humans have resorted to manipulation and trickery like diverting messages or freezing the brain now of we ask what happens is that humans

How To Find All Missing Persons / Unsolved Cases. And Collect All Reward Offers.
Volume XV. THE CASE OF GWENNETH GRAHAM

in light of this case there has been significant changes to the normal and usual ways this court look at cases for the first time we have nothing at all to identify the killers therefore all we did was to ask the force of gravity go look at this case for us this is what he said if i look at this case as i have then the killer is atern stopntopsr who jumped in the air and said i slash for my own house they slash lives we slash victims and they slash houses what a deadly combination identified as william tin mathsters who was 19 at the time who said i am tired of being pushed around so i search how to kill and never get caught i asked aty why every crime is easily solved and he said they followed all predefined guidelines put in place by god and they always solve a case and i said remove all predefined guidelines what do we have he said nothing an unsolved case that will last 20 years and a huge reward because none of the people they employ have iq greater than 100 mine is 1100 that's a whooping 10 times that of humans now why humans iq is just 100 why mine is 1100 is because i think above humans any formulas i make no human will ever solve for 1000 years so what do you have in mind he said i want to kill a person so easily and watch him die with that person not even attempting to save her life how can i do this above all without even getting caught now ask what can be of humans that kill and never get caught and it said they have iq greater than 100 that means they can easily solve a case and can easily make things harder for those who solve cases remove all predefined parameters and you literally removed all humans from the case remove atmospheric pressure and you are left with a situation that needs only gods to solve now remove planets now you have things only god can solve now what exactly do you want i can write the most difficult case to solve i can say what was and want can never be and get the facts of the case then go on to create the most difficult case to solve even if you know the killer but how do you prove it in court we must therefore asking the gods a question what is the most difficult case you have ever solved in the entire history of the world and the answer is the case of estelle estuve who was murdered and the killer stayed there all night asking what can you see and removed all that so that what is left is just a corpse that can't be asked if you do then the case is

How To Find All Missing Persons / Unsolved Cases. And Collect All Reward Offers. Volume XV. THE CASE OF GWENNETH GRAHAM

thrown out for tampering with witness but only in examination and autopsy is tampering only that humans have no way of talking to dead people than i do now

what his aty said was that if humans can't solve cases humans committed the can they solve cases the gods commit it's common sense they can't that means think like a god and solve all human cases now what needs doing right now he said i want to disable all warning system with a slash and remain so calm that everyone also remains calm that she won't react at all until i say die where she must easily fall and die so how can i do this it sent him the answer through a bundled nerve bundled that embeds and expand the ideas so that only him knows what to do now humans have become so clever that they can replace everything the court use to judge cases with almost nothing so that so that they test how the court is carried out we have send now let's see what this boy had in mind and list everything he did

1 he disabled the send.ya messages
2 he cut off electromagnetic waves from going to the souk by slashing at a precise angle of 33 degrees the trajectory of death by design now if we ask why this is the answer at 33 degrees the blood flow is restricted to outward movements alone that means less inflow hence lack of electromagnetic waves to the brain now if we ask what could be then this is the answer the brain can only deal with what is at hand if electromagnetic waves are insufficient then the brain can't process some of the commands like activate the switch of death now what is left is for the soul to escape and tell Yahweh what happened but of this does not happen then what happens is that Yahweh must use the atmosphere to find solutions but what if we remove the atmosphere to find solution then he must use the gods us as the council of creation now what can be said of all this now humans ate getting understanding of what happens then what can be done of the gods now in this case Yahweh use the force of gravity to identify the killer who he said was atern stopnosr who said if they can and getaway with it i can and slashed her now what can be said of this atern stopnosr he is a ruthless killer nevertheless he can make mistakes he did not

How To Find All Missing Persons / Unsolved Cases. And Collect All Reward Offers.
Volume XV. THE CASE OF GWENNETH GRAHAM

understanding what is removing atmospheric pressure he could have said gravity don't interfere mass don't judge and air don't breath during my acts only for next 10 mins they would have agreed now let's see if that had happened what was the next stage the court was to use to judge these cases next was Yahweh with his geographical positioning system that identify.
to conclude we must find other ways of finding the killer other than gravity as used in this case his results were that atern stopntopsr killed her after asking his aty what was the best was to kill a person and get away with murder how did gravity identify he used time and electromagnetic waves which are 89867890183867890189286783t867890123678901283687898201 84 identified as atern stopnosr real name martis mutervnop who killed a one gwennth gavvino graham using a sharp blade remington steel aktprst 7868 which he bought outside a garage called aster ssterss which is on highway 286283 status us that he is alive releasing more electromagnetic waves current location is 88687898286878901838687801248790183867890 11 south of australia looks like in a caravan or small accommodation out of nowhere his phone number is 83687892848678912386789012389 0286 australia use the first 12 digits

gwenneth gavvino graham a click activated only at steropqstuvwxyz meaning st garage road was etersotpmnopqrst meaning stopotev in australia at exact 22.06 pm but everything stopped soon afterwards meaning either instant death or disabling of systems die to lack of electromagnetic nerves now what we know now is that he used removing of everything using an angle of 33 so that first she can't remember him or his friends when he goes to hell that means instead of the usual predefined of
1. tell us how you died
2 tell us who killed you
3 tell us who and when this happened extracted from the predefined parameters afterdeath for humans
now what happened is a tragedy because this woman is just coming

from work when these attacked just one slash from their leader at 33 degrees killed her removing all atmospheric but the killer misunderstood the meaning of the removing of atmospheric pressure so that only the gods can decide it that means humans can now think as the gods and above the gods
the end.

THE KILLER, THE CONFESSIONS AND THE COORDINATES

 Now I remember I am also gwenneth gavvino I had no son but pretended I had one I had raised so much money over the years that I bought a second house and put it in a name I just faked on account that no one will coincidentally come and say I had a house and was his what are the chances and now what happened is that I raised 823648 dollars from locals over years as a cheap hooker and over years I earned more than most of the people in power but where do I keep all this information I thought why not buy a house iand hold it then change name in the future and sell it I have receipts etc then a police man called Simon terps said good morning miss where is son and I said mind your business you retetetetet meaning useless rat and he said h and has a house worth 2832869 in that name but without any documents and he asked his aty how he can take that house and it said not a chance she can easily change her name to that ne and claim everything within her entitlement but unless if she dies before she changed name this was on 10 August 1974 at the police station in the city of perth on that day an asm automated sign message was sent to a one stern ajern who said if they can what makes me fail and how his aty said if she said Pc Simon terms says I own a house in another name and ended up dead
Simon terps bought a house once owned by gwenneth gavvino^{o}þ Graham who was found sexually assaulted with no leads bought that house from the ceterts house for 82384 only when it once had a value of 28368973 a fraction of the value.
atern stopntopsr killed her after asking his aty what was the best was to kill a person and get away with murder how did gravity

How To Find All Missing Persons / Unsolved Cases. And Collect All Reward Offers.
Volume XV. THE CASE OF GWENNETH GRAHAM

identify he used time and electromagnetic waves which are 89867890183867890189286783t867890123678901283687898201 84 identified as atern stopnosr real name martis mutervnop who killed a one gwennth gavvino graham using a sharp blade remington steel aktprst 7868 which he bought outside a garage called aster ssterss which is on highway 286283 status us that he is alive releasing more electromagnetic waves current location is 88687898286878901838687801248790183867890 11 south of australia looks like in a caravan or small accommodation out of nowhere his phone number is 8368789284867891238678901238 90286 australia use the first 12 digits
gwenneth graham a click activated only on at steropqstuvwxyz meaning st garage road was etersotpmnopqrst meaning stopotev in australia at exact 22.06 pm but everything stopped soon afterwards meaning either instant death or disabling of systems die to lack of electromagnetic nerves now what we know now is that he used removing of everything using an angle of 33 so that first she can't remember him or his friends when he goes to hell that means instead of tge usual predefined of
1. tell us how you died
2 tell us who killed you
3 tell us who and when this happened extracted from the predefined parameters afterdeath for humans
now what happened is a tragedy because this woman is just coming from work when these attacked just one slash from yheir leader at 33 degrees killed her removing all atmospheric but the killer misunderstood the meaning of the removing of atmospheric pressure so that only the gods can decide it that means humans can now think as the gods and above the gods

EXTRA INFORMATION OBTAINED USING OTHER METHODS LIKE THE DIGITAL ELECTROMAGNETIC WAVES FROM PHOTOS

who killed you
martis murtevnop a local kid from house 832867890 i walk past that

How To Find All Missing Persons / Unsolved Cases. And Collect All Reward Offers. Volume XV. THE CASE OF GWENNETH GRAHAM

place everyday and see him sitting outside he always say i am hungry where i get food hey grumpy mrs can i and touch his penis now what can this real me about him he wanted something other than food my aty said he wants buttfuck according to your aty who killed me they all did matis slashed you on your chest i knew you would die because my long ago started as well at 22.08 a minute after yours meaning only death and mine said if you can scream scream now and let's see how clever you are can you run away or you are going to die as well and say lack of electromagnetic waves when matis strikes he waited exactly 8 minutes for you to collapse before the others started attacking but with nothing just between legs fighting saying you should have accepted the 400 dollars but he said she would have turned us in all of us that was her task as well it's not who got killed its who was first i can tell you why i killed her she was assigned to kill all of us by lethal injection or in prison tonight was the night she was supposed to hand us in imagine if they are desperately for money do you think they prefer one small house the size of me kitchen or three houses all owned by orphans now if they want us then who best to put us behind bars her she said i will ask one if he want sex if yes i give him once and put the others behind bars but if he wants money then i will walk away and sit when i sit you must also sit at home and say where are you and call me once and live the line open if i pick up then everything is okay and if i don't then come running because i will be in trouble all have aty and these little devils say everything the don't have secures brain power is she didn't finish as her son said no i can't be there for you if you try to do that to people of my age so i refuse if they find out it's gonna be trouble for me so to love me i won't come so that means don't go and don't expect me and that night i passed by the house and stabbed him hard 8 times to represent 8 times i can miss my own house payments as he died he said i die spare my mum who is going to take care of the house and i said i will today i am you and you me the killer i will carry you after tomorrow and bury you at the cemetery where anton sevretnson was supposed to be buried and you shall be in that hole forever so he took the house papers and put in his name and said i will own both houses sell mine and stay is

How To Find All Missing Persons / Unsolved Cases. And Collect All Reward Offers.
Volume XV. THE CASE OF GWENNETH GRAHAM

his son until when god comes to find out
jamie mum help someone in the house with a knife
jamie
i died mummy i was killed by a house breaker who said if they can i can unless if God comes and said 33 degrees and i freeze he slashed my neck and said tell me a story and something seemed to have stopped and he said can i c keep the house and i said what he said okay i can keep the house so sign i thought i agreed and signed he then slashed me again and again counting saying i miss i lose the house you miss you lose nothing but this time you lose your life
if god really knows he will
digital electromagnetic waves identified for a one gwenneth graham sexually assaulted by atrop amnesia and atrop atonp real names jame storpnsorm 19 and   aklmnop rstuvwxyz meaning ztelty who was 18 after another called matis mutervnop said if they can kill and get away with it why can't we and slashed her once after being talk by his aty at house 8238678 he knocked the door on 27 september 1974 and said if they can why can't i and slashed him in his throat and said 33 for 2minutes he said tomorrow's i come and bury you at the cemetery as anton mutervnop and said
code 8768983867892841089838678901836289102386 was used on her just before the attack by pc astern ajern real name in case of gweenth amtop anopqrstuvwxyz meaning stuvwxyz meaning deterst who sent a message saying in case god might remember you by thoughts you had before this is to make sure that god cannot identify you if he did then you will be lost because he will know we want your house in the name of gwenneth gavvino graham using three names to defraud us his electromagnetic waves is pc atopq surname could not translate but gave sturvwstop and followed by another suggestion stuvwxzy meaning
create antidote for code 8768983867892841089838678901836289102386 created and its 8238689877801982831748699102867809832101890 lift all restrictions put by man
electromagnetic waves
8986778899283489280184982786778890123498018234867890 18

How To Find All Missing Persons / Unsolved Cases. And Collect All Reward Offers. Volume XV. THE CASE OF GWENNETH GRAHAM

3 he said if god knows the truth and is a real god then he will simply find out that this gwenneth is also the same gwenneth gavvino who owns a 3 bedroom.house in same street of these boys because she goes there to sleep after pretending to leave with a man aternpqrstuvw also known as atrup who said if she can then i can and ask everyone for a cut to pay rent for sex now if i can then everyone can does that mean i am god because there is nothing godly about god hiding when people are dying in fact i am going to hide and say i killed all can i have a bonus then went for all for their houses one by one starting with that one with the eyes of the devil matis murtevenop who said i can if they can because i just say houses to houses ashes to ashes and get all three houses and get a raise then wait for the reward say all the correct phrases and get all the money unless if god is found ..
Pc atorp mutervenop lifted the fridge and put it next to her body so that it stay fresh as much as it can because if she can't be recognized then the house will be taken by the housing association instead of the police if that happen there is no way to prove that gwenneth Graham is also gwenneth gavvino meaning a crime of fraud hence a crime scene otherwise abandoned houses don't follow under the jurisdiction of the police but of the housing association proof she got killed for the house and he is the same policemen who bought that house and who is expecting the reward.

...I found God...visit www.twofuture.world

THE CLAIM

the reward offer

9fds
THE COLLECTION

www.twofuture.world/donate

ABOUT DAVID GOMADZA

visit www.twofuture.world

signed david gomadza
ask.davidgomadzaauthorised.licensed.checkya.askya.ya

27may23.42pm
scotland
00447719210295
davidgomadza@hotmail.com
info@twofuture.world

How To Find All Missing Persons / Unsolved Cases. And Collect All Reward Offers.
Volume XV. THE CASE OF GWENNETH GRAHAM

How To Find All Missing Persons / Unsolved Cases. And Collect All Reward Offers.
Volume XV. THE CASE OF GWENNETH GRAHAM

www.ingramcontent.com/pod-product-compliance
Lightning Source LLC
Chambersburg PA
CBHW031515210526
45464CB00007B/2924